In *Texases* . . . the vision of his land is as real as mesquite debris or a governor who *jogs just down the road / with a pistol for coyotes*. At the same time, it is ethereal, entering poems visited by angels and biblical cadences and scriptural tones. Indeed, it is everywhere. Poch creates this landscape and its people with skill and beauty, in a voice that combines wisdom and humor, enlivening a book that is a joy to read.

—**GRACE SCHULMAN,** *Without a Claim*

Like the *staked plains, dry-land, long view man* he praises in one poem, John Poch knows the harsh beauty of Texas, and in this new collection he gives us a plural, abundant portrait of his beloved place. Here are prose poems, sonnets, villanelles, and all the enduring pleasures of formal verse, brought back down to earth by Poch's unflinching eye, and his hard-won knowledge of work, and people, and the past. Texases is a kind of psalter, full of graceful and moving love songs to the land.

—**PATRICK PHILLIPS,** *Elegy for a Broken Machine*

TEXASES

TEXASES

POEMS
JOHN POCH

WordFarm
SEATTLE, WASHINGTON

WordFarm
334 Lakeside Ave S, #207
Seattle, WA 98144
www.wordfarm.net
info@wordfarm.net

USA ISBN-13: 978-1-60226-022-1
USA ISBN-10: 1-60226-022-2
Printed in the United States of America
Cover Design: Andrew Craft
First Edition: 2019

Library of Congress Cataloging-in-Publication Data

Names: Poch, John, 1966- author.
Title: Texases / John Poch.
Description: First edition. | Seattle, Washington : WordFarm, [2019] | Identifiers: LCCN 2018055905 (print) | LCCN 2019000596 (ebook) | ISBN 9781602264298 (ebook) | ISBN 1602264295 (ebook) | ISBN 9781602260221 (pbk.) | ISBN 1602260222 (pbk.)
Subjects: LCSH: Texas--Poetry.
Classification: LCC PS3616.O28 (ebook) | LCC PS3616.O28 T49 2019 (print) | DDC 811/.6--dc23
LC record available at https://lccn.loc.gov/2018055905

P 10 9 8 7 6 5 4 3 2 1
Y 24 23 22 21 20 19

ACKNOWLEDGMENTS

Agni: "In the Backyard after the Dust Storm, Meditating on Paradise"

Alabama Literary Review: "Ransom Canyon"

America: "The Rio Grande (South)"

Birmingham Poetry Review: "Windy Day in Flower Mound"

Blackbird: "Independence Creek"

Bliss: "Metaphors of Lubbock"

The City: "Psalm in a Desert Place"

The Common (online): "God in the Shape of Texas"

The Cresset: "The Neighbor" and "Our Flesh"

Ecotone: "Late Afternoon at the Junction Rodeo"

Gettysburg Review: "The Gate"

Grey: "Texas"

The Hampden-Sydney Poetry Review: "Love Creek"

Harvard Review: "Lubbock, 1955"

Hayden's Ferry Review: "Mason Mountain"

Ink & Letters: "Horses and Sawhorses"

The James Dickey Review: "Playing Hello Kitty Bingo Before the Merit Committee Meeting"

Juked: "Texas Hollywood"

Linebreak: "Off the Grid" and "The Dallas Cowboys Cheerleader"

The Nation: "The County Seat of Presidio County"

The New Republic: "The Llano River"

North American Review: "Horse Crippler *(Echinocactus Texensis)*"

Orion: "Hill Country Drought"

The Oxford American: "Cowboys vs. Texans"

Pleiades: "Pegasus"

Poetry: "The Llano Estacado," "A River" and "Good Year"

Scythe: "Big Bend"

Sewanee Review: "Crush, Texas" and "Loving and Goodnight, Goodnight and Loving"

Shenandoah: "The Brazos"

Smartish Pace: "Great-tailed Grackles"

Southwest Review: "Punctuation on the Devils River"

Thrush: "Escape on the Sabinal"

Unsplendid: "Invisible Fish"

The Well Review: "Texas, Apostrophe"

Yale Review: "Evening"

"Watching a Train Pass, Denton, Texas, 1:35 A.M." appears in the chapbook *In Defense of the Fall* (Trilobite Press, 2000). "Lark Sparrow" appears in *The Poets Guide to the Birds* (Anhinga, 2008). Some of the poems concerning rivers appear in *Between Two Rivers* (TTU Press, 2019), a collaboration with photographer Jerod Foster. A grant from the Scholarship Catalyst Program at Texas Tech University allowed me additional time and space to complete these poems.

for my parents

CONTENTS

III.

So I arose and went out into the plain, and behold, the glory of the LORD stood there, like the glory which I saw by the River Chebar; and I fell on my face.

—EZEKIEL 3:23

You are Texas, the old man said. I was Texas three year. He held up his hand. The forefinger was gone at the first joint and perhaps he was showing them what happened in Texas or perhaps he merely meant to count the years.

—CORMAC McCARTHY, *Blood Meridian*

TEXAS

They made us come out to the country to this ranch. The moon rose. Probably full, it was orange and squashed, some kind of optical illusion because you could see so far on these plains. The others were excited. They pointed at it, jabbing and saying, *Look. Look* is something we might say when we mean *listen.* Coyotes suddenly howled in the ditches a mile away. Everyone looked at each other, wide-eyed and smiling. And then another group of coyotes a mile in a different direction. I believed it had little to do with the moon and much more to do with the sandhill cranes that had alighted in the cotton fields nearby. The ache of hunger. The moon kept rising and lost its orange, and those around me couldn't get enough of it. The moon was a wheel of cheese, more moldy as it aged into its great height.

No, that moon was an old god occluding all those stars and satellites and planets. The others wanted the formidable plot, and I wanted the simplest verbs. The stars, as that nonchalant white nightmare rose, the stars were blotted out one by one, like angels God grew weary of. God doesn't tire of angels, but this is how I felt. I would compare the whole scenario to a video game against the work of a good day. What did I want out here in the great wastes of the plains? Stars were a sure thing, and I couldn't do a thing about their disappearance. Everyone was happy for the moon. The holy white buffalo of it, baffling the world. Whereas they felt it to be the coziest of comforters, I needed distance on it. I wanted the piercing diamonds sprawled across black velvet. Listen. Instead, because of winter, there would be a full twelve hours of this awful silver coin hanging itself.

I.

GOD IN THE SHAPE OF TEXAS

Imagine something lifeless as a road
even makes meat for the crooked crow
or a necessary perpendicular walk on the caprock
without barbed wire might have made a man
a man from the expanse. And that man post-holing
could feel freedom's labor in his molars—
could see the cedar post would one day boast a meadowlark
like a trophy of Western flight.

Five strands strung hip-high help God help us,
and the triumph of the cowboy boot is up there
with the bullet. Don't holler till you shred your palm
on a twisted star or dig your heels into the real
of a stubborn bull. Iron in the hard times may rust
but waits, patient. No one around here talks of centuries.
In January, Esperanza sobs at the Texas Proud Coin Laundry.
In February, the cranes tend to settle on last year's cotton.
In March, the John Deere green erupts like a shout, by God.

Verily, who can resist the tiller we call sand fighter as wide
as the Second Baptist Church? With this sun, who could resist
buying a hat? Across the purblinding aluminum desolation
of the football bleachers of Paducah, Texas, the wind
howls, of course, and there goes the first big tumbleweed
to mar the new truck out front worth half the house.
You can't go far before you find some corrugated metal
leaning, leading to a brick downtown, the Masonic flourish
of God's compass hung on the one impressive building
near the stoplight. On the outskirts, some dream of a boxcar
in their own front yard, a walkway of cement pavers

in the shape of Texas leading to the porch around the side.
Texas. Texas. Texas. Texas. Texas.
When even children recognize the figure of an angel
rising from the Gulf of Mexico, panhandle-headed
in humility, they pledge allegiance to her flag,
the white star silver in their eager eyes, postures
simple and fixed as any town's water tower,
and as proud, and under God: Look up.

THE DALLAS COWBOYS
CHEERLEADER

When the Cowboys cheerleader cheers
for a body, it is her own in blue and silver,
like a dove thrown into the sky fleeing gunshot
successfully, arcing her torso into a holy spirit.
Her athleticism is nearly unimportant.
She is the reason they make lipstick
into the shape of a bullet.

COWBOYS VS. TEXANS

Last century, like angels before the world was born,
Cowboys ruled the West. Now, like angels scorned,
come the Texans to lay the black on blue.
Partner, that's not face paint. That's a tattoo.
Houston's bigger when you measure earth;
but Dallas just might circumscribe Fort Worth
and then lay claim upon America besides.
Who can seize the year? a star? these bragging rights?
A cowboy often plays the lead, the hero, loner,
calling the shots, misread, in trouble with the owner.
And the symbol of a bull skull doesn't take college
to understand—they sacrifice the body. The knowledge
of good and evil goes down pretty ugly in this Western.
Arm-chaired, steady as a pump jack with that beer, Texan,
throwback-jerseyed, deep down you're old school—
deep down an Oiler, dualies in the backfield, diesel-fueled.
Or classic silver-blue the color of the propane hour.
Frack the whole state, and choose your power.
Know your basics, the chalk of X and O on slate.
If Emmitt Smith was free will, Earl Campbell is your fate.
Pick longevity of a consistent arm and the vain
over the new old running downhill on a level plain.
Or blitz the patriotic red, white, and black
over our Republic's model quarterback.
Have faith; the ruined knees are good for praying.
It's Sunday, after all. Who works? Who's playing?
How does the hour empowering us turn into three?
All three sides of the ball—the postgame trinity.
Michele Tafoya, tell us if you know the story
when the MVP gives God the glory:
the camera finds the other, the cloth upon his head
almost hiding the grown man crying, broken in our stead.

DON'T MESS

This Texas woman is a threat . . . or fun,
her little T-shirt tempting: COME AND TAKE IT.
The image of a cannon helps to make it,
black star between her breasts, her hair undone.
But is she packing heat, somewhere a gun?
Does she mean to mock you, make you see her naked?
She looks you in the eye and wouldn't fake it.
Her secret weapon isn't set to stun.

The both of you are married, so forsake it—
this independence—pluck out your eye and run,
remember Alamos or wars you've won.
The light that blinds undresses everyone.
Leave Texas lying; one misstep can wake it.
The diamond warns: you better (she can) shake it.

OUR FLESH

Boring as a vulture shadow, occasional and reliable,
maybe a blink which surprises, the flesh tries.
And here we are again sweating
by the buckets or by the pool, in the flesh.
Yet might we want a nice nest despite heaven
and, like the great crested flycatcher, weave
a sloughed snake skin in to make fun of sin?
Snag it from a cottonmouth whose head newly shed
waits like a god or a hood ornament, king of macadam,
pretend friend to Adam, hell to the pygmy mouse who
at night makes a little pile of pebbles and each morning
licks up the dew as some of us drink bitterly our coffee.
These days we are all connoisseurs of drought.

On a walk through the dust after breakfast, I imagined
a cottonmouth coiled and lost in thought like a pretty girl
curled up on a couch, awash in TV. But then the dream
turned, and I saw the snake levitate in the humid blue
of the Hill Country sky, hanging there, so I thought
I should destroy it, and then I thought of the scripture:
a cloud the size of a man's hand rising from the sea.
Was I imagining the end of days or the prescient end
of the year's drought here in the dull apocalypse
we call the flesh, the sad fact we call the world, 2020,
coming year of the hindsight?

Cheer up. We don't need nature's illustration.
The flesh is a fine hotel for love, if not a temple
where you can come and fall on your face
before a seemingly empty throne.

OFF THE GRID

While our governor jogs just down the road
with a pistol for coyotes, I like the outdoors
for the decorated meadowlark on the barbed wire
above three horse cripplers. He teaches me valor
in patience across the cirrus-strewn morning.
Sleep low needy needy moving, he tells me.
I have lost my wallet I know not where and may
yet find it, Lord willing and thieves be damned.
In a world of hurry's fistfuls, the thorn of money
obstructing nearly every ordinary path like mesquite
shoots waiting for a snag of feather, fur or flesh,
I'd like to bushwhack the clumpy field a mile
and, at worst, make a bird change direction.
I best appreciate the science of a parking lot
from here. In his famous way, death outlives us,
or so he thinks. Our governor, he must think of me
what deer think of the cows, compatriots of the pasture,
one group swifter, perhaps, though not a little daft below
the corn feeder, or what anyone ponders driving by
the Boston Terrier Museum, Floydada, TX.
Yet what can I do when God votes for me?
I must love the governor, my enemy of education.
The opposite of war is eating, so I will now cook
my dinner on a fire, while he awaits his pricey dinner,
and know he is nearly my poor father,
and both of us suffer, one perversely,
the frail imaginings of a country king.

SUGAR LAND BARBECUE

The Italian word for picnic is picnic.
The same in Spanish, in French, in Japanese.
What else would you call it?
In Texas we call it a barbecue
and spell it with three consonants.
The pot-bellied host shall provide a meat
and may just cook it in the ground.
Who wants cake when we've got cobbler?

Lulls will befall the barbecue, such as
the one after the argument about arguments
that hung between the husbands and the wives
precarious and flimsy as a badminton net.
Then a beer can cracks things back to bragging.

There is always a woman at the picnic,
though you may have missed her bear-brown eyes,
who sulks at the periphery, lonely as a picnic table
at a junkyard, balancing a bitter can of beer
in one hand (as it warms and is not drunk)
and a magazine somebody asked her to hold
in the other. Look how she so wistfully
looks at the house finch on the backyard wire
singing a tune like a string of hard candy.
Its voice and its color cheer her
like cherry cobbler does the others.
Nevertheless, she withdraws around the corner
of the garage to her car. She will escape, but first
she soaks up the heat and stillness of the dash.

TEXAS, APOSTROPHE

Your solipsism loves the sunshine, so you
smoke Oklahoma all morning like a brisket.
In the windbreak shadow of a double-wide
fifty miles due east of the lower Panhandle,
a dusty yellow butterfly battles the gusts
on behalf of another wild onion flower,
an odd morning front backbuilding to the dry line
raises its jackrabbit ears, remembering softball-
sized hail.
          Texas—like a hawk's beak
tired of taking comfort in its own shoulder—
you could assault me, but you don't. Instead,
your warm spring storm may bring quick rain,
a downpour to strain a tea of tumbleweed and iron
in the gulleys where the whitetail worship gray
till they bound forth flashing their false surrender.

Exasperated by rifles and the coming night,
coyotes complain as sharp as teeth on tendon
and flatter the spread with their best questions.
Their ancient eyes shine back bloody gold
the glare from the new oil rig lit up till dawn
like a monument to God's insomnia or what
the mammalogists and kindergarteners call
the nocturnal. Fuel fuels fuel, we say,
and the hardhats eat breakfast before bed.

Our farmers tolerate breakfast and the forecast,
then turn it all under from a great green throne.
Cisterns wait at every turn, and the turns are far

and wide, while what mesquite survive hate height,
all branch, hate trespass. The shredded remnants
of an armadillo at its northmost border testify:
The sky. The sky. The armor-piercing suck of sky.

TEXAS HOLLYWOOD

—Almeria, Spain

Bored as St. Sebastian with all those arrows,
a reluctant teenage boy, dragged by his father
and duties of the holidays, feels *nada.*
Good thing I'm not there to not go, his brother
texted from the States, *STAY in Granada?*
Europe's only desert? No gracias: he'd rather
the blood and sequins of the *toros'* eros.
No shade from either side of the thoroughfare
right now, high noon, this blinding glare
the reason for broad-brimmed hats, boleros,
and a street oriented South South December.
All this dreamlight nothing to remember.
The red sand underfoot puffs fine as flour.
He leans his back against and rests his arms
on the crossbar of the hitching post an hour
in an anti-ecstasy of false alarms.
Even he knows the prancing Andalusian,
its neck reined back like a tower of blood,
is no cutting horse, the art of the rider less illusion
than the fronts of the one-street neighborhood.
A rooftop cowboy bellows English, but not:
Choose between bread or a dead dog! A gunshot.
The only cloud in the sky is this odd cloud
like a bleached human femur floating on end.
From a roof falls a man in love with dust.
Then oblivion of a horse bolting away. Disgusted,
the boy aloud: *Is it over? How far to the bus?*
If you're walking, says a pretty girl behind him, *I bet*
as long as it takes to smoke a cigarette.

THE LLANO ESTACADO

How much soil do you plow to soothe a conscience?
If you're a staked plains, dry-land, long view man:
a sky's worth. Some even sow the dry playa
midsummer with sorghum, the cotton plowed under
after early hail. Thus, not every farmer keeps
an old broken homestead sacred as a graveyard.
Today, no sharp-shin on a pivot for an omen,
no stoic farmer on a turnrow changing water.

Among a little wind grit, in a grid on a grid, somewhere
like the crossroads of outer space and Earth, Texas,
a handful of ragged elms withstands a long sway
of heat and wind. These old guards of a home haunt
the field but wither as even ghosts must. Honor them
with a walk among homesick bricks, and prophesy good.

GREAT-TAILED GRACKLES

Trying to leaf, the one elm
in the field near the prison
is a verb. All the grackles
at sunset in this bare tree
face west as if listening
for the vatic goodbye
that is my fate on the plains.
It's only the wind
that makes them turn.
They face the wind.
The field is cottonless, accused
by white windblown bags
and occasional Styrofoam,
the early spring grasses
bleached and blown low
already. A wooden ladder lies
by the tree near the road
at the edge of the empty field.

RANSOM CANYON

in memoriam Robert Bruno

I. Lake Ransom Canyon

Two rows of western soapberries line the road
to a stop sign before you drop into the canyon.
What leaches from elsewhere, the bright green lawns,
from the maze of predictable brick homes built within
and on the canyon who adores only erosion?
What from the cotton fields, the gins, the sorghum,
prairie dog dross, the power company,
from the feed lot bovine-crush slogging through
their excrement up and off the rim? It turns this water
green-brown-gray as a dying fish, as crumpled money,
a steady cloudiness like the sore eyes of the very old.
After a rain, stand above the long spillway
and watch the smooth sheet of water suds
at the bottom of the concrete fall and funnel
below a barbed wire fence a cowboy repairs
into the North Fork of the Double Mountain Fork
of the Brazos River.

II. The Chapel

The curve-billed thrasher at the chapel perches
among the orange berries, wary of cats
and bold coyotes. Hold still and you can hear
the water trickling down the arroyo to the pond
above the other artificial ponds and,
ultimately, lake complete with geese.
Here, Comanches traded their white captured

to the comancheros who, in turn, would turn
their profit. Now, the realtors flip the houses.

III. The Party Island

The flagpole bangs its flagless rope
in the wind. The derelict, rusting swingset
and the empty swimming pool dismal
between two yellowing cottonwoods
say goodbye to summer. On the long dock
lies one abandoned Zebco rod and bird's nest reel.
The island clubhouse, full of metal folding chairs
arranged to face the western end, is ugly enough,
aluminum, a roof, and big on echoes.

IV. The Robert Bruno House

> More music, really, than sculpture.
> **—ROBERT BRUNO**

Like the dark head of a dead goddess
rising from the orange crumbling rocks
and caliche at the edge of the north cliff, the house hovers
        as if to judge
the dam and her lake. Instead she sings stained glass sonatas
        in her head.
Rusting steel sheets by the hundreds held by welds of
        decades of bending
and a lot of horsing around are skin and skull to a patient labor,
        a library
in the dark core whose several lamps we must imagine.
        If you were to wind
on staircases in the wind ushering up from the canyon floor
        to this edge,

turning on that steady stair like a vulture to her evening
        perch at the rim,
you'd want this steel to hold like old poetry, the window
to cast its eye over and into
the old spring-fed ravine it misses.

THE NEIGHBOR

Forgot to say hello to my neighbors.
Sometimes I question my own behavior.
—**JOHN MELLENCAMP**

I.

Across the street, the 1960s blond brick wall
behind where the honey locust used to grow is all
too bright. Now, the neighbor's tumored tree
hangs like a silhouette in memory.
The phantom limbs hang like a daylight moon.
But drowned in the light of Tuesday afternoon,
nothing is harder than this brick. I don't know
my neighbor. The tree service workers hauled
the dead limbs with the wilting fans shattered
and waving away last Friday. The blind wall is all,
whose one dynamic is the gutter-spatter
stain along the lower third. The slag lake
and dust of the bark left floating in the wake
of Friday's trashy truck and trailer are the opposite
of the trail left by an animal as you hunt it.
The wall says, *I told you so,* torso and tower
over the summer-scorched yard and looking away.
The wall almost supervised as the tree was stifled,
unspanned limb by limb over the span of an hour,
as the tree-men hustled and regarded each other
with the masculine disdain of a feminine trifle,
strutting their work, extending their arms
in a display of veined limbs bristling
and the possible violence of the living. Harmless
behind the blinds, I kept my distance.

II.

A fascination with suffering has me
watching, by turns, the kingbird smack
and smack a cicada against a wire above
the street to my right, and then before me
on my wrist, the one size-sixteen gray mayfly
in Lubbock, Texas, alights. This is early August.
My stationary mayfly is august and tough
with no trout stream for hundreds of miles.
And the cicada, but for her sheer sheared
glistening wings in a rudderless helicopter fall,
is a waste of thirteen dark years at the roots
of the tree now gone and hauled away.
Nature's overrated; the wall calls.

III.

My house shadows my neighbor's house.
The mayfly, tiny ashen dragon, sails away.
The neighborhood's earless cat, whom I call Ears,
has come around to sulk, his wary head
the softest softball of shame. Not a mouse.
Not a mouse in the house, he seems to say.
Not hear. He spooks and disappears when I move.
I come to the stump, finally, not to find
my epiphany, but to stand on it, to bend
over it, amused at a minor kingdom fallen.
This wall's windowless, and only the stump
looks up with its worm-hollowed eye.

No one's home. In my neighbor's yard, I stand
for nature. I shrug. I lift my hands.

WINDY DAY IN FLOWER MOUND

A cardboard box lid tumbles down
the street. On a wire, a starling shakes
and shakes its wings and screeches
like a toddler tottering on a pool edge.
Below all of us something
is dark as a crankcase.
The cat-head irises rot their skins
and veins all over themselves.

Am I unhappy? Who cares?
The irises are as exhausted
as spring-sick starling chicks
just spilled from eggs, drunk
with light among some fumes
of blue-green leaf and stem.
I wrote *trust* on my arm.
I haven't prayed in two days,
and confession is me
writing that down, or pride.

The flood aqueduct beyond the trees
and scrub rushes with rainwater.
In it, the paper boat
of my imagination is tossed
across eternity's subdivisions
until I wake to find
the starling flown, perhaps
to the moody saxophone of an estuary.
He will sing to his home
as I sing to mine, his dull wings

the brass tarnish of a spit valve.
Sometimes I am not even a starling.
I am an immature blood platelet
waiting for a wound.

HORSE CRIPPLER
(ECHINOCACTUS TEXENSIS)

Not only
your nearly scentless
floral remnant is persistent.
Your fruit, globose, spiny,
nested on a thorn-crowned
gray-green brain, each
kinky-pink pinball,
if uneaten by coyotes,
will dry to a shriveled
red rattle for
a baby devil's hand.

Gorgeous in a bad way,
your thirst-fueled inch-long
lowest goat-horn thorns
want to pure hurt something,
years waiting for that
frenzied charge of hostiles
up from the Trans-Pecos.

I have been this angry
on packed, dry dirt
among loose stones,
lifting my upset head,
broken down, rooted,
as I am, to a dearth
and a wealth of flat earth,
the party again parlayed
to *thou shalt not,*
in a farm road bar ditch
while clouds fire west

along the dry line looming,
and I witness the front,
dark with an anvil
lording over it,
O Lord, Thou Fire, Hammer
of my edge and purity.

CENTRAL TEXAS

I was in a funk
last night, a little drizzle
patter on the solar panel,
and now the front speeds to the east.
This morning heaven has stepped
so sexy from her drab shower
that well under their rocks
the rattlesnakes ache.
And last night's little rain
nudges a honey-green lift
from the meadow
reaching to kiss her blue father.

Truck-size piles of mesquite wreckage
across the pastures rot
like the best sins gathered
together into the worst sins.
They take a while, but
thank God, they rot.
Mice make kingdoms here.
The kestrel applauds one stack
after another, not seeming
to tire. Speaking of, the wind
blows in the stovepipe top
above me like a preacher
from a long ways off,
silly, but right this time, on fire
like a voice out of nowhere,
from on high: *The kingdom*
of heaven is at hand—
you'd better listen up.

GOOD YEAR

January. I pluck it,
this feather flapping
in the bare mesquite
only head-high, caught
by the down. Iridescent,
turkey. Another feather
in the bleached Texas
gramma and another . . .
A coyote somewhere naps
happy, grinning like
the feather evolved from a leaf.
What luck.

Clouds lift above the field
as if to swallow my eye
into hunger. Good hunger.
The greatest eye must
behold me like an ember
dropped into a finch nest,
and I smoke at the mouth
like a gun dreaming in a safe
of a war it can win by virtue
of its praise. I have lost
the great phrase I concocted
on my country walk
with the feather in my pocket.
I cock it.

IN CORPUS CHRISTI

The church has a different take
on the body
than the rest of the world.

And the gulf fixed between
the two is unbreachable,
though we try like lovers.

In the morning the children cry out
in mostly pleasure along
the miles-long beach,

interrupting love and rest.
And the rest is love
and relentless sun.

Beneath this beach umbrella,
in my head I'm making a map
of the month of June.

Kids out of school
and wild, dig the legend,
and X marks the spot.

By three, leisure's lethargy
spills rainbows like bilgewater
from an aircraft carrier.

The trudge up to the condo
is a journey to a nap
and strange waking to drinks.

Evening along the pier, and
the sun goes down while the moon
comes up. Gold and silver.

Few who built these miles of sea wall
ever measured moonlight.
And few measure it now,

though I get a little romantic
and also hope for a small hurricane
against the piles of seaweed.

CRUSH, TEXAS

William George Crush conceived of a train wreck as a spectacle. No admission was charged, and train fares to the crash site were sold for $2 from any location in Texas. About 40,000 people showed up on September 15, 1896, making the new town of Crush, Texas, temporarily the second-largest city in the state.

     Why don't you put on that antique swallow necklace
    before you dress and come downstairs for breakfast?
   The one I got in Spain. Not quite precious
metal, but the Deco style curves the edges
  and softens patinaed bronze and the swallows' restless
    flight on delicate porcelain, the nexus
      of breasts, our hearts, our corresponding sexes.

     The thought of that pendant makes my hands nearly reckless
    for balance, to become the ambidextrous
  beloved who loves to lose at Os and Xs.
Our children sleep. Come down. Come here. Perplex us
  with swallows, voracious with your reflexes,
    with the crush of you in the terrible state of Texas
      that like a staged train wreck (in a good way) wrecks us.

LATE AFTERNOON AT THE JUNCTION RODEO

Where the sun is not silent
but crackles white like spit
on the tips of my yellow teeth,
spit thirsty for bourbon
while thistle pinks and fizzles white
on the far periphery, even
the bleachers are beat from waiting
to catch the glimmer of a last spur
thrown skyward to goad the day.

We're not piñatas, yet why,
while headed to the truck,
do I feel so suddenly silly,
hollow, so colorfully tattered,
hung and stick-struck, swung,
gaping at the air of settling dust?

The patience of the live oaks
bordering the parking lot
sickens me, their growth slower
than a lesser-known old Western,
the dull plot of blighted acorns unfallen,
fused by rot to the branch tips,
by blue and yellow lichens,
these false-green, heat-cussed ornaments,
here on the cusp of summer.

Though you are lean as winter wheat
and lovely, your cotton dress is frayed
like the fins of an old catfish,
my collar's crooked, and our children,

full of sugar they believe
will always fall from the sky,
spun from steamy clouds of cotton,
have invented a game called
Stomp The Shadow.
It's my turn, and behind my back,
they shuffle their little boots
upon a semblance of my head.

HILL COUNTRY DROUGHT

Despite the prickly pear anchored
in the crook of the old pecan
parched and sprawling in the high branches
like nature's monster ears hanging
on any word of man's frail failure,

and despite ten thousand catkins curled
and desiccated in the half-
hearted shade of the noon pasture
grasping at the absence of grass,

in this stricken field
two invisible angels have concocted
a game with painted buntings.

They toss them from crippled mesquite
to old mullein flower stalk and back,
and those neon bouquets even sing.
And sing to the new mullein leaves,
soft as the ears of sleeping deer.
And sing *Happy Birthday* to the dust.
And sing *fire fire where where here here*
to the reluctant cuckoo who brings
his three big gulps of water.
Please pour it in my ear.

IN THE BACKYARD AFTER
THE DUST STORM, MEDITATING
ON PARADISE

—Lubbock, TX

After four months without a rain, each step
puffs bleached grass chaff and dust around my shoes
and, this afternoon, green is a far ship kept
at sea. Last summer's sheets are far, the news

of rain in the radio forecast before we'd rise
for coffee and toast. You walked toward this same sage
bluer, then through the dew, the lawn disguised
in mercury. We were a different age,

a different couple altogether. The constant
in us is faith. As far as this dust above
my ankles is from one of your dew-wet footprints,
this is the distance between human love

and paradise. Can all begin with a garden
and end with linens, music, laughter, water,
each neighbor passing bread, wine? Someone—*Pardon,
but she is pretty. Is that your wife or daughter?*

PLAYING HELLO KITTY BINGO BEFORE THE MERIT COMMITTEE MEETING

My daughter, this ripe apricot, this living
number four, this delicate jar of flowers,
eyes that softly lash the morning green,
like waiting for a rhyme, she takes
her time here on the oak floor after breakfast.
Her hand in the velvet bag delays,
dramatic as a rabbit in the depths of a hat.
Her eyes closed, she must imagine her choice
of one of the last ten of these little tokens
could awe princesses and then haul up the sun.

It lays a door of light across our knees
to open morning further on its hinges.
She calls herself the candlelight maker. And me,
I am beard baby. I am so sorry silly.
Too, I am an old man who is not old.
When she finally pulls from the velvet
her sneaky arm, she delays, and then,
my pyrotechnical machine of bubble gum,
she turns her pink hand over.

But I clasp her hand with both of mine,
and we hold still like three houses of hands
around a mouse who might escape.
We crush. We are quiet as a jar of flour.
She doesn't understand the symbolism
of a door of light minutely moving on the floor.
She doesn't care for incentivizing service
and doesn't grasp, like us, the sad term, *research*.

To win, she just needs Joey. And I need Lorrie.

I know the difference between Joey and Lorrie.

WATCHING A TRAIN PASS, DENTON, TEXAS, 1:35 A.M.

The click, the click, the constant song of wheels
abates. Gates indicate *OK to go*
by lifting like a referee reveals
a score: *It's up, it's good, I say it's so.*

The windows haze inside because of cold,
and I can make a little footprint with my hand.
Look through it here, and see how streetlamps hold
their cones of light above our own waste land.

Your olive irises go gold, sublime,
street-lit, gazing down the barrel of a lane
prepared for love made of the inquiline.

The wrong side of the tracks just asks we thank it
before we gun the engine. The silo sign
in neon lights goes: CORN-KIT, BIS-KIT, PAN-KIT . . .

THE BRAZOS

Below the Possum Kingdom Dam,
this stretch, like a housewife
toward a happy anniversary, hurries
certainly, knowing how steadily—
far but sure like an ocean
gussied up with palms and mangroves,
anhingas patient on cypress knees,
phalaropes anxious for circles,
in circles—fate waits.

She has encircled me
with her bare arms, and her eyes
don't worry like a canoe
tied to a river island. Her eyes
are wet and quick like a swallow
skimming the river with a little splash.

In shadow the wind on water
over white rocks moves light to delight,
and just downstream around
the next bend, high-tension wires
hold above the scene. They travel
to a hospital and to houses—
one house where a woman
irons shirtsleeves smooth
as the arms of God.

THE COUNTY SEAT
OF PRESIDIO COUNTY

One thinks of boats this far from water
then goes back to just-so crushing into sculpture
the rear and forward quarter panels
of three cars pasteled for half a century
by the Big Bend sun, by the windy grit,
tarantula spit, and even piercing starlight
for that singular space in the mind of art:
an abandoned barracks in afternoon's half-shadow.
Even in winter, it's a long way for the glare
to chariot his old welder across the sky.

Boyd Elder sweeps the wasps from Prada Marfa
a good twenty miles from Marfa proper.
Someone else hates that someone by accident
swept the Russian schoolhouse everyone loves
to hate. A colossal horseshoe crucified
with a ridiculous man-sized nail against the sky
casts the shadow of a sickle and hammer.
Yuccas lean for decades, and the rust on all
maybe-likes the sun. After a downpour flees
east to Alpine, best to shake your head
at the green that almost tries. It didn't rain last year,
and it won't rain this year, says the mayor
to the hung-over travelers who could be artists,
and one of them writes this in a notebook
for an angel he saw late last night down the long
Judd-red counter of the convenience store,
her entire right shoulder's agave-blue agave
tattoo lit by the cash register candy-bar light
where she bought cigarettes as they locked the doors.
Who could know she would come all this way

with her soft bangs, her confident nostrils,
and that utterly touchable old white sweater?
He hopes deeply she might run him over
with the land yacht of her prevailing aesthetic.

PSALM IN A DESERT PLACE

I lift my voice unto the hills
where there are no hills, perhaps rises
where they bulldozed a homestead,
my voice torn among the cedar
windbreaks, hung up, strung out
like spent shotgun-shell Christmas lights
the locals strew with what decadence
or what abandon they can muster.
Smile and say, *To Kill Ya.*

What little rain falls makes
an inch-thick paste of caliche on my boots.
The shovel underfoot and in my hand
has a voice like horse teeth eating sand.
This nexus of my Texas exile,
this burying the family dog in sand
and limestone, strains and stains me.
Suddenly, the Busted Triangle Ranch
seems symbolic as do the three hearses
yesterday in the Allsup's parking lot.

My voice would move a mountain
to where there are no mountains
and would not cast it into the sea.
Daydreaming the sea, I feel what
the dog must have known when I played
for her my recordings of coyotes.
O, for only the grassy dunes
of my childhood vacation by the sea!
O, look, a baby javelina skull.

LARK SPARROW

Let me be drawn to you
and not the elusive yellow-billed cuckoo.
Rather than the colorful dozens feeding
in the understory of the broadleaf trees,
specifically the villainous red-eyed vireo,
I prefer your symmetrical beak
navigating the side-oats, your chestnut cheek and brow,
the white around your slick black eye.
Yours is a Clark Kent cheer, or a purer sorrow.

The swallows with their shining superhero-purple heads
ride their invisible roller coasters, ridiculous all day,
and the wrens ascend and descend like nervous angels
their ubiquitous ladders, while along the river
the supercilious kingfishers complain.
But you, my nearly unadorned, you shun the coasts
and line the cup of your well-made nest
with grass and one sun-bleached straw wrapper.
You sing on your low perch when you are satisfied.

Enslaved to your plain behavior,
how could I forget you choose to share
the field with me? You choose the earth.
Let the earth be dust beneath our feet
and each occasional flight.

LOVING AND GOODNIGHT, GOODNIGHT AND LOVING

These roadside Western placards shade the blind,
bleached turf that blinds a history. Someone's keys
might rust out there, lost, prairie-buried, might find
no mechanism spurring sweet release,
no purchase. What's the purpose? To unlock
the joy, but more the wandering grief, station
yourself like some poor town's long depot, chock-
full of childhood's golden dust motes. Prize privation

at the Ranching Heritage Museum: Less
is. Thirst would always map the trail. To win
was to, despite the sun, refuse undress-
ing till night, good night, keeping the moisture in
and loving the distance like nothing. Keys,
no need for keys. The Pecos brings us to our knees.

THE LLANO RIVER

In a pile of mesquite debris in the field
not far above the river, a cotton rat twitches
in its sleep, dreaming of a sharp-shinned hawk.
Down near the river bottom, the giant stands
of pecan trees canopy a trampled deer path
which is its own small stream carried away
with her footsteps. The wind moves through
the grass at the bank like three deer, and then
three deer move through the grass like light wind.
They are three does the color of rotten twine,
and they lift their heads when a single mesquite leaf
shakes loose from its tree fluttering as if
it had wanted this long spiraling downward.

Her path leads from the field to the river,
and I have followed with my book in which
none of this appears, not one wooden giant
or a path or a woman I must follow with my book.

HORSES AND SAWHORSES

—Mojácar, Spain

I.

Morning lifts the mist while Andalusians
whinny furiously afar their controlled
and hysterical cries. I have seen one
step and prance her rider nowhere,
the neck rippling a wet leather color trained
by leather in a famous, furious arc,
the polished neck as formidable
as the flashing shins are fragile.
Eyes of lightning, thunder in the breath,
this horse can lord it over the beach
or above the lake in the mountain,
knocking down the stars with her hooves.

II.

The rickety sawhorses bearing
a seven-foot length of plywood
make a table for spreading out
a book of poems page by page.

The sawhorses lift an infinite plane,
a level by which the world is measured.
God taunts Job with a vision of a horse.
I hold my breath lightly like the reins.
How can I magnify the Ancient of Days?
My lines lie trampled like grass where
deer lie down by day. And it is night.

PEGASUS

Anyone might imagine a horse in flight
when thrown from a startled animal with the brain
of a bird you thought might know maybe a bite
about the bit in its mouth and your sure reign,

but from your newest vantage point, wounded,
legs turned to salad, dust your saddle there,
you can witness from the depths, grounded,
the wild mane and the holy hooves in air,

a white bonfire against the heavy blues,
see nostrils flared and lording over the riot
of a man who thought he'd write a poem, pretending
to ride on anapests over horseshoes . . .
while poetry muses on the fallen poet
watching a horse, white as a wave, ascending.

BIG BEND

The clouds hang on the mountains
like coyotes on barbed wire.
But then real entire coyotes drape
these fences like thunderheads upside down.
The clouds loosen, the coyotes sag.
And in the evenings, howls from the mesa,
the smell of wet dust and sagebrush.

LOVE CREEK

Is there water better than secluded creeks
where cold springs rise in warm late spring through layer
on layer of limestone rock? We hide and seek
the real Hill Country south and find the prayer

of solitude we need. The overflow flattens
wide as a Texas courthouse, a flat dime deep,
like a Slip 'N Slide for giants. Nothing happens
for a hundred yards, but then, my love, Love Creek

narrows, tumbles, and drops to a cool pool
where, ahead of you, I place on the darker sand
an invitation, a limestone chunk (I'm a fool
for signs) I found: a heart the size of your hand.

You descend the trail like the song of a canyon wren
and smile at my offering. We enter in.

EVENING

Does love covet
a reflection,
or is it one night
that in its eros
outshines the sun?
You can look out
the window
easier than
you can look in.
The force of the sun
lying down, day,
is almost over now.
Shadows stride the land,
tipping a balance
of fear and peace.
Classes on doubt
are offered here
by the rising
weight of blood.
Wait. Time, plural,
is what we might
call evening.
Stay in. Come out.
The neighbors have
televisions.
There is a window.
There is the moon.
The world is in-
consolable,
and this is why
you look back in
at where you were.

III.

A RIVER

God knows the law of life is death,
and you can feel it in your warbler neck,
your river-quick high-stick wrist,
at the end of day. But the trophies:
a goldfinch tearing up a pink thistle,
a magpie dipping her wingtips
in a white cloud, an ouzel barreling
hip-high upstream with a warning.
You wish you had a river. To make
a river, it takes some mountains.
Some rain to watershed. You wish
you had a steady meadow and pink thistles
bobbing at the border for your horizons,
pale robins bouncing their good postures
in the spruce shadows. Instead, the law
of life comes for you like three men
and a car. In your dreams, you win them over
with your dreams: a goldfinch tearing up
a pink thistle. A magpie so slow
she keeps even death at bay,
she takes her time with argument,
and hides her royal blue in black.
Shy as a blue grouse, nevertheless God
doesn't forget his green mountains.
You wish you had a river.

THE RIO GRANDE (SOUTH)

Cascabel of liquid days
weaving inaudible Zs
in your long slow passages,
where your scales
weigh in the balances
the light and grays
reflecting quartz and dust,
how do you fuse
two visions into one tongue
forked now and then
with such thirst
wandering through
this long brown chasm?

With rain you might wake
and wash the foothills,
for heaven's sake
rolling over stones,
the ocotillo jealous
of your distance, the roots
of juniper and willow
reaching to touch
the ragged hem
of your garment.
Iridescent,
as if risen,
you leave behind
your holy ghost.

ESCAPE ON THE SABINAL

Like a river, we flashed and flooded to schools
toward some imagined paradise, as yearned
our own kinfolk who fled their parents' rules.
We were exactly right to go! Those fools
can't see—for us, back home is where the heartburn
is, was, where romance is a butter churn.
Humidity of the Texas Hill Country cruels
the summer days with sweat while winters earn
their solitude. Cold almost freezes, cools.

So girls became our toys and books our tools
at college. We learned to judge the jewel
God is, saw earth's insides like Jules Verne,
and Eden lost was not so bad. Adjourned,
we had traveled East!—But snow . . . helped us discern

we missed the constant sun, the heat, affirmed
the good of cypress shade to rest our souls.
Too hot? Stay still until the evening fuels
a breeze. We know now we didn't know, confirm
this thread might lead us to original pools
where we might lie among the spring-fed ferns
and watch for the orangest orchard orioles.
Our canyon loves; the city ridicules.

To fish, as well as fathom we're food for a worm,
is to accept a river's unconcern—
how it surrenders water molecules,
and rains, drifts, calms, distills, reflects, unspools.

We leave as soon as we can, only to learn
we spend our whole lives trying to return.

INVASIVE SPECIES

Some days are better than others.
Yesterday, from a helicopter, I slaughtered
with an AR-15 a couple dozen wild pigs
for miles along a desiccated river.
Nowhere to hide, they fell like dull dominoes
on the limestone bed and dust, with little puffs
of exhaust where the lead goes through.
The biggest boar, tired of the metal god
of constant thunder above, tired
of his own old fat and heaving tusks
that he would have loved to sharpen
on my thigh bones, he tried to hide below
a thin mesquite he considered a tree of life.
We chuckled as righteous God must have
at modest Adam in his sin. *Where are you?*

We lit up his little Eden with the angel of death.
They tell me any wild pig over a year old
tastes rancid no matter how you cook it,
ham or loin or meaty shoulder. Some say
it tastes like human flesh, but who would know?
You couldn't hear the laughter over the roars
of all our hovering power poured out.
I admit we paid a lot to get those kicks
and free beer at the cabin after, watching
the sun set. Later, someone by the fire asked
a question: *What is the glory of God?*

PUNCTUATION ON THE DEVILS RIVER

An hour off the paved highway, you have to take
a washboard dirt road past unattractive cactus,
sage, and cedar scrub, and miles of hapless mesquite,
until, after a few long barren washes, a river
in this wasteland overflows, and religiously
a thicket of little sycamores lets a lot of green light in.

We ford with a pickup the long, flat, fat limestone shelf.
Up the bank in the oaks, asterisks of parasitic moss
like old, blind eyes just watch as we unpack.
The dark, little goodbyes of yesterday's rain
fade in the distance, move over another ridge,
another county, another heaven, under God,
divisible by doubts and wants.

Now the wet wind of low clouds racing boredom
and erasing mediocre plateaus tries to hide
four aoudads scampering the sheer rock face in mist.
This mist rises, and collecting drops seep down.
The biggest millipede in Texas, more than
the span of my entire hand, drinks tenderly
at the edge of a pool of dew, slow as a plateau crumbles.

At Dolan Falls, the shapely shelves hold
a different kind of book, limestone leaves whose language
erodes with the dew of ten thousand years.
In this month of May, ferns emerge in every crevice.
On a long flat shelf, three *tinajas* punctuate the morning
like nature's ellipses refusing conclusion,
and their distilled reflections of clouds lift.

Let's not be too tender about Texas.
Water penetrates stone to death and dissolution.
After long droughts come floods,
and another limestone shelf the size of a tugboat
chases a giant white padlock in a Dali dream.
Suds below the falls the wind pushes
back upriver like dull weather memories.

And finally, the upside-down exclamation
of an angry smallmouth leaping for a moth
seems as possible as ice cream to a cowboy.

I wait on the comma of a big river eddy
like an eye waiting on light behind a black shutter
hopes an explosion will fall into an image.
I am always wanting that black aperture
of my form to flower geometrically empty
until I'm nothing and you are all. Period.
And like a psalm God swallows, I know
what light knows the Devil doesn't.

INDEPENDENCE CREEK

Down around Independence Creek, the plateaus below I-10
are all the same height. If you take a photograph from the crown
of one on a humid day, the air is so white, my friend,
it may seem someone has cropped the entire top of the terrain,
and that right there is Texas sky so clean and long you disdain
the roof of your house and any shade tree that may
hinder heaven. Between the plateaus lie mostly mesquite
and prickly pear and a billion centipedes in a rarely wet May
crawling between limestone scrabble and coyote scat.
Drop down to the valley floor, and up from Caroline Spring
comes the clarity of a smallmouth bass and his tail waving
a black flag like a lazy dog waiting for small trespass to raise his ire.
The canyon live oaks are few and far between except where
the springs and creek can keep alive the struggle and grip.
The low clouds of morning scud along like ghost steers
drifting in search of grass until, at its height, the sun is a whip
and makes of the wind a long fire to purify the idea of distance.
You can't measure the gratitude of the Proserpine shiner
in the shallows of the impossible water praising the Refiner
in the Chihuahuan Desert limestone stretches and big vistas.

THE COLORADO RIVER (TEXAS)

for Keith Rodgers

Close to Lampasas on one half-mile stretch
in early March, the water clarifies
almost. The mountain laurel purples sass

the rotting browns of winter. You think you'll catch
not fish so much as a God who loves disguise
and a great spill of tea with milk—and pass

the boredom, please—with gray skies dropping mist
then spitting rain. And cold, you realize
you forgot your waders. You wade and ache. You cast,

surprised by the strike, the electricity-kissed
white bass.

INVISIBLE FISH

The guide at the slideshow asks us
who can see the fish.
Each, in our own Alaska,
could guess, but only a wish

we could be surer rises.
Reluctant to raise a hand,
our total silence comprises
our mute self-reprimand—

an ax-headed thought might swim—
a stone mistaken for a trout
below the ruffled scrim
of the run would leave no doubt

how Texan, how far we are
from mountains. The hush confirms
our ignorance: we'd mar
the world with hooks and worms.

His silhouette's afloat
behind the projector's boulder,
light swirling hotel motes
before him: silt, lit golden.

If he's the fisherman,
then we're the fish aware
of shadows, movement on
the shore, hunger and fear

our needle north from birth
and sex to death. He waits
as patiently the earth
holds steady on its plates

till a laser pointer now
points *fish fish fish,* discloses
how wrong we were from how
we hid within our guesses.

The last few slides, and on
come the lights. The river
evaporates. We're gone
like fish out of water shiver.

METAPHORS OF LUBBOCK

On Avenue F, pigeons besiege french fries.
They are like the women on a smoke break
outside a metal door at the gas company.
Full of hankering, they chat, and condemn men
and yesterday, and let their cigarettes ash
and ash. We are far from love.

The women look up. The corners
of the buildings are griffinless.
One woman's brain feels to her
as dry as this sheet metal.
She could complain at any moment.

Yet, the sheet metal, from afar,
in the orange light of a windy late afternoon,
is like an orange detail
of a color field painting
by Frank Stella at MOMA.

Frank Stella, with his shaped canvases
of unremarkable colors and his parallel lines,
is like the father I never had.
The father I never had is my father.

LUBBOCK, 1955

Back when Buddy Holly first invented high school,
the principal proclaimed it from the podium.
The chemistry teacher gave a slice of sodium
to every boy with a playa lake or swimming pool.

Something in the aquifer or the Lubbock Lights,
and the Monday backyard Ping-Pong tournament began.
The home-ec teacher casseroled her lesson plan
and made out with the baseball coach post-Friday nights.

The remnants of the cotton crop windblown from trailers
drifted pretty at the edge of town like snow.
Our grid of streets named after other cities, though,
was windswept clean as any Midwest minor failure.

January and June, a boy named Elvis played
his part to frame the spring semester, and, in between,
senioritis burned in nearly every teen.
Then summer came, and James Dean died. Undismayed

by fall, the birth of rock and roll was our new knowledge.
Toward winter, the girls wore sweaters soft as malted shakes.
When the mascot fired his gun for real for heaven's sakes
and terrified the Muleshoe Mustangs, he felt like college.

LUBBOCK UROLOGY

for Chris Brown and Howard Beck

The art of losing makes this kind of poem.
But, be a friend, don't toss my kidney stone.
I want to meditate on it at home.

This concrete pain—I want to be alone
with it as one who polishes his chrome.
The art of losing makes this kind of poem.

In Emergency, I lost all words except this drone:
an urgent, deep-seated religious ohm.
I want to meditate on it at home.

When sore, we feel much better when we moan.
Exactly why do I gnaw this meatless bone
the art of losing makes? This kind of poem,

unless the words dissolve, cannot be known.
Especially the lines I chose to clone—
you'll want to meditate on them at home.

Remember, in the end it's all on loan.
Thanks for getting me going, flowing and flown.
The art of losing makes this kind of poem.
I want to meditate on it at home.

SONG OF TEXAS

after Manuel Machado

Marfa—a mile high almost.
Dallas, the death of JFK. Fort Worth
and stockyard boasts.
Houston's where we exit Earth.
San Antonio ghosts.
Weird Austin. Lubbock, we lament in
and rock and roll.
And Denton.

MASON MOUNTAIN

The mountain must erode
from wind and rain washing away
the soil, plants, and rocks grinding
themselves to dust to make
a fertile valley. And the animals
below who eat the grass and mount
the heights for a change of scenery
or safety, a view, build,
with what they carry, the mountain
back. Though all comes down,
the wind will carry up feathers
and rain containing particles
of smoke and nitrogen, spider
and seed against the wrench of gravity
and death. Sometimes a hundred slaves
will carry the soil aloft with bags
upon their backs or barrows,
constructing terraces, fighting
the loneliness of sheer rock God
calls up from underground to sky.
Or the Devil trying to push a stone
against the sun. Mostly it is made
with solitary molecules in time
blanketing a peak, accreting
for a tree's sake. Years, and on it
a hawk watching. You see,
this tree is like a cross,
and the hawk's talons
are clenched as if nailed there.
And her ancient longsuffering eye
more than an imitator of all
she knows that came before.

THE GATE

That year we summered in another state,
between a mountain and the mesa, in a house
behind a house amid *acequias*.
When I asked if we should close the gate,
the owner said no need, don't worry, but
she would close it anyway (the last one in
most nights) because she liked to.
Something about this Taos-blue metal gate
on its rusted hinges swinging shut.

We fed our infant daughter Cheerios,
fruit on the tip of a plastic spoon. Mornings,
I read—two books on love, two more on war,
some poems from the shelf by Yevtushenko
by sheer coincidence—coming to few
conclusions. But one night, post-flamenco
on the plaza, the sunset in the cottonwoods
like a temple flame among some ancient pillars,
we rose, walked to the car and headed home.
Instead of a last turn left toward the willows
that the Rio Pueblo watered, I turned the car
toward the sagebrush mesa. The sun had dropped
behind some pink and purple virga. Rain
on one dry valley—it seemed real rainfall fell.
Raising a cloud of dust, I hurried us,
worried we'd miss some bruise-strewn turquoise blue
and clouds cartooning bloody, final thoughts.
On Blueberry Hill, I pulled to the shoulder.
In the back seat, my wife began to nurse
our daughter. I lowered the windows first,
got out, then forced my camera's aperture
upon the scene, as if a lens could hold

the total moment as one might try to capture
a sunset with the rind of a tangerine.
I put the camera away and let
the heavens do their work. We weren't late
after all, and while some clouds would rapture
into nothing, others darkened, and others
over-ripened like forgotten fruit.
When the darkness finally descended,
a raven silhouetted into view
before us on an updraft, mended
the night like a crucial needle passing through.
I drove us back to our temporary life,
our home for now, the summer's flight. My wife
took our daughter in. Can you see me hesitate,
when in that dark I tried to love the night,
the stars, far seeds of faith? I closed the gate.

AMARILLO RAMP

Always wanting something like balance,
weighing on us; they are the reason
for harbingers. And they are chosen,
the living, the best we can expect
in this world. They make us cry more
than the dying. They make a ruckus
and take a long time to learn to walk.
We have to wait for them to keep up
in cemeteries or any earthwork
as if they all were elderly.
The good thing about the living
is that you cannot make them alive.
Their inconsistent work cannot
be measured with scales and clocks.
With their black coats and white collars,
to ascend they must descend first.
Full of feeling, a part of nature,
malleable as earth, hemmed, warmed
by the painstaking order of their play,
they believe they know what they do.

BIRTHDAY

December, and the sandhill cranes
are circling overhead,
invisible as stealth jet planes,
their harmless cries widespread

on silence. They have the sense to know
that south is safer, warm—
behind them rolling hills of snow
and next year's farm after farm.

They circle and complain somewhere
a mile up. You have
to crane (haha) your head and stare
a stretch like a giraffe.

And finally you see the line
the thermal draws them to.
That straighter wind, the sign,
invisible and blue,

above this Texas college town.
Adrift, they look like gnats
got organized and made a frown
or a smile. Their habitats

remain as long as cotton fields
are farmed, or corn, or sorghum.
At night, they hold the useless shields
of their breasts, silencing their boredom

in hopes coyotes won't surprise
and leave them in a heap
of feathers torn, legs strewn, orange eyes
bewildered beyond sleep.

Or morning, they rise from earth, away,
ungainly, lucky, like me,
below, surviving another birthday,
a cancer scare. It strikes me—

I'm loved despite my gazing toward
the mirrors of my days.
Forgive your selfish servant, Lord,
bemoaning holidays.

Though discontent and fickle, I
can turn to a ballad, tropes
of seasons, turning birds on high,
and open my envelopes.

I know the New Year is just one
more turn toward death. O life.
My cake and candle-fire come.
We sing. We take the knife.

ABOUT THE AUTHOR

John Poch has taught in the creative writing program at Texas Tech University since 2001. He also serves as series editor for the Vassar Miller Poetry Prize at the University of North Texas. Born in Erie, Pennsylvania, he earned an M.F.A. from the University of Florida and a Ph.D. from the University of North Texas. He received a "Discovery"/*The Nation* Prize in 1998, he was the inaugural Colgate University Creative Writing Fellow in 2000, and he was the Thornton Writer-in-Residence at Lynchburg College in 2007. During 2014 he was a Fulbright Core Scholar to the University of Barcelona.

His collections of poetry include *Poems* (2004), a finalist for the PEN/Osterweil Prize; *Two Men Fighting with a Knife* (2008), winner of the Donald Justice Award; *Dolls* (2009); and *Fix Quiet* (2015), winner of the 2014 *New Criterion* Poetry Prize.

His poems have appeared in journals such as *Agni, The Nation, New England Review, New Republic, Paris Review, Ploughshares, Southwest Review,* and *Yale Review.* He is a founding editor of *32 Poems Magazine* and a co-editor (with Deborah Ager and Bill Beverly) of *Old Flame: From the First 10 Years of 32 Poems Magazine* (2013).